Winner of the L. E. Phillabaum Poetry Award for 2016

GOD'S FOOLISHNESS

POEMS

WILLIAM WENTHE

Louisiana State University Press
Baton Rouge

Published by Louisiana State University Press
Copyright © 2016 by William Wenthe
All rights reserved
Manufactured in the United States of America
LSU Press Paperback Original
First printing

Designer: Kyle Peyton Bonner
Typefaces: Minion Pro, text; Goudy OldStyle, display
Printer and binder: Lightning Source

LIBRARY OF CONGRESS CATALOGING-IN-PUBLICATION DATA

Wenthe, William, 1957–
 God's foolishness : poems / William Wenthe.
  pages ; cm
 ISBN 978-0-8071-6245-3 (pbk. : alk. paper) —
 ISBN 978-0-8071-6246-0 (epub) — ISBN 978-0-8071-6247-7 (pdf) —
 ISBN 978-0-8071-7248-3 (mobi)
 I. Title.
 PS3573.E565A6 2016
 811'.54—dc23
                                        2015022023

For Jacqueline and Sophia

"Now, I say . . ."

And for three teachers:

Peter Quinn
Michael Tobin
Dominic Garvey

Because the foolishness of God is wiser than men . . .

—I Corinthians 1:25

CONTENTS

I.

The voice said, Cry. And I said, What shall I cry?

—Isaiah 40:6

The Call

Mid-August, and that barely perceptible
tilt in the weather, the slight stepping-back
of sun, hinting of the season to come.
My late-night walk to clear another day's
reckoning of things done, or supposed
to be done, or only hoped, when I hear
a call that comes this time of year, whose source
stays hid in high branches, or higher—
perhaps some night migrant's sporadic cry.

Clear, sweet-toned, but impossible to say
whether four short notes, or a single trill.
Then silence: the space the call had filled,
for a moment, returns to the same leafy street
I walk, past darkened windows; but knowing now
I'll hear it once, maybe twice, a night,
well into Fall—a sound forgotten
most of the year, until one night it comes,
that call, and the question, *What is your name?*

Parable of a Birthday

A man comes to the town of Artesia . . .

So might begin the story of my coming here,
since something about a birthday wants
to seek a shape in time, the gift
of a symbol. This town lies between
Loco Hills and Hope, between oil and water:
gushing wells that first brought farmers here
floated a rainbow stain, a faint whiff of tar
that lured the wildcatters in to drill.

Driving in from the east, it's oil and gas rigs,
steel orchards among red sand and mesquite;
signs that warn of poison fumes, too small to read
while driving past with windows rolled up
against the stink of brimstone.
Then, lording over the entrance to town:
the oil refinery's reeking, throbbing riddle
of pipes and valves and ladders.

Farther west, a spring-fed creek
waters a narrow valley. Apples, pastures,
trout in the dimpled current. Deer will come
to the bank, at dusk as I make my last casts,
and drink. Though in daylight
it's cows, or the signs of them, I'll see:
grass trampled to mud, or turds
glossy and black as creosote.

Come nightfall I return to town,
a motel room with a carpet
that blackens my socks, a view
of tank cars in dark procession.
Can something be made of this refinery
besides oil? Can that ever-burning flame
atop the exhaust stack be seen
as the Purgatorial "fire that refines"?

4

So much of what we do
with what is given—the raw resources,
water and oil, apple trees—amounts
to shabbiness . . . like those fences mended
with doors and hoods of cars
scrapped on the farm where I fish.

And so I am come to Artesia,
fifty-one years after the day I was given
birth. There's a stuffed, two-headed calf
in a storefront window looks both ways
down Main Street: mildly interesting,
of no perdurable meaning, but enough
to give a moment's arrest, to say
without words, *You are here,*
and here you are. Roughly.

A Cedar in Paris

So this is what it was to be born—
to be dropped into a scene that's been happening already,
utterly without me: afternoon winter sun
ladles through cloud breaks, rolls on the Seine;
and the walls of the Louvre inhaling with light
like memory; behind me, the hotel where Voltaire died,
and under that green water somewhere, lie
his sculptures an enraged Modigliani
heaved into the current. One of the rare gifts
of middle age—to know a little something
about a place where I'm arriving, as if new born
but with a kind of memory, a recognition,
a haven't-I-seen-you-before: why, here's Verlaine,
glowering in stone in the Luxembourg Gardens,
and a pigeon dozing on Apollinaire's head
carved by Picasso in the churchyard of St. Germain;
here's van Gogh remembering a painting of Millet,
and here's Millet's painting, recalling a noontime haystack nap:
all these memories not mine, but ones I'm stepping into,
like the hollows troughed over centuries
by bootsoles in the stone stairways.

When I was 23, I stood on the stone floors
of Mycenae in moonlight, having snuck inside the walls
after closing; and I roared aloud the choruses of Aeschylus
in the chambers where the very murders occurred.
Now, these low buildings at home in the rain—
these metal roofs rounded like upholstery,
rows of windows tall enough to take in
the city they partly describe, their cast-iron balconies—
invite me to play a simpler role, of mouthing the words
for street names I've read, in novels and biographies.
Even this walking is styled
with precedent—Was it Baudelaire who coined
the term *flâneur* for the stroller among galleries
of sidewalk and window, grazing on the details?

And the details continuously tongued and discussed
in the daily gossip of weather: cobbles
silvered after a rain, stained-glass light
evanescing on walls, fading as clouds
nudge the sun; a pollard willow with a blackbird in it, and then
a pollard willow without a blackbird in it.
So, jet-lagged and needing a nap, I'm delivered
to my own life seen newly,
in a city whose memories were old before me,
in the gray-misted otherness, gargoyled and ordinary,
of what-is-given, that relentless destination
of our constant arrival, the only place
I'll ever write my name among the tombs—

here in *Père Lachaise*, in another turn
of the weather, I wedge the spokes of my umbrella
among cedar branches, so it hangs there, a makeshift
shelter where I smoke my pipe, and waiting, watch
a little brown bird they call a *grimpereau*
probing the papery trunks of cedars: a curious
engagement I've entered into, this moment
of no other history but this,
among monuments of the dead, their names dissolving in rain.

Monuments

The slow archaeology of melting
snow discloses a forgotten
sandbox shovel, garden hose nozzle,
department store flyer heralding
a one-day-only sale. When I find
the tea mug I'd left outside,
steeped now in snow water,
it looks (or seems to look at me,
as I recognize that chip in its rim)
surprised at having been
neglected beneath the snow.

Archaeologists in the early days
mainly sought monuments;
now it's the ordinary stuff,
the tossed away, they attend to:
the people they're looking for, like us,
living among the very things
we daily hold and lose
even as we're holding out
for more, for some great,
winged, human-headed bulls
marking the entrance to some
storied city of one's own.

Principal Events—that's the heading
of the list Paul Roget began
at the age of eight, ransacked
by his father's death. Eventually
he came upon the idea
of listing ideas: arranging all
the coil, moil, intrication of living
into transcendent categories—
a monumental list
he named for an archaeological
term for "treasury."

There, my overlooked tea mug
half-filled with snowmelt
is raised up and restored
as *mug,* and received
(along with *noggin, nipperkin,*
and *gallipot*) into the receptacle
of *Receptacle.* But there, too,
the singular objects
are scrubbed down to
universals, forgetful
as the covering snow.

And even if Roget's intention
is sacred, herding all *Existence*
into his thesaurus's
ultimate entry, *Temple;*
there's an older story
of our own limits,
and that story still requires
the snow, white as the garment
Jehovah wore, to melt again
into mud, admonishing me
with the vision of that mug—
that mug I call "left handed,"
because of just where the chip
on its lip is placed.

A Lesser Story

My trouble with the historical dead
is the way they always come to us
complete, fledged with full résumé
of deeds, each one a tableau of self
accomplished: with palette or sword;
wearing the iconic headdress—tricorn,
black beret, coonskin cap, or crown

of thorns. Yes, you. More than anyone,
you've been given to me since childhood
as alpha and omega of fulfillment:
magical babe printed on cards, perfected
sufferer nailed above an altar,
never far from the beam of light
that overwrites all wounds with
the happy ending of The Greatest Story . . .

And your nonchalance of loaves and fishes,
your hem-of-the-garment lauds
for others' modesty—even in humility
you are pedestaled; and how we reverence
your wrath that rectified the temple.
I gave that one a try, not long ago:
called out the hypocrites, manipulators—
the money changers, so to speak,
in my place of work. What a supreme
failure that was—they only fattened
on my fury, and I became the fool.

But now that I am washed in
the abrasive eyewash of humiliation,
I think I can see you, thoroughly
stripped of your story. As for being
endorsed as the son of God, I wouldn't know;
but haven't we both understood
how it is to be spurned by *persons,*
to be called *poser?* Surely I've never been

scourged as you were, but I believe
you might have felt, beneath the blood
inflicted by whips, the seep of your own,
self-generated, sweat of unworthiness.

And would you know then, too, the feeling,
the tempest within, of not knowing
who you are? Lord—Stranger—
stop with me here. Let's grab an empty table
and meet: you, me, some wine,
and the unstoried pain
of becoming man.

Junkyard

I don't know where it comes from, the absolute
certainty with which my daughter declared
that boys do not wear bows, as I clipped the scarlet bow
to her forelock, then wiped red glossy smears
from her chin and cheeks, thinking: might as well
give a four-year old a flamethrower
as give her a tube of lipstick.

Driving now to the auto salvage, I recall,
as new parents, our expectant delusions: *Oh,
we'll be better than that,* we thought; *we won't let
such gendered pressures distort our little girl.*
And just as I once tried, absurdly, to teach her,
three years old, to make a fist, and take no shit
from that bigger toddler in preschool,
so I want to tell her now, *Look darling,
I've lived in the West Village, and I'm here to say,
if a boy wants to wear a bow, just let him be free
to rock it as he pleases.*

But already the old show's begun:
how I'm secretly proud for knowing
the backroad shortcut to the junkyard—
a man who's been there, knows his way around;
even as something in me cringes
because I'm only looking for a small part,
the cap to a coolant reservoir, to fit
my Volvo. I can almost hear the yard man think,
'What's that, Mary, you say a *Volvo? A station* wagon?'
—as if his camo coveralls and steel-toe boots
require him to think that; which only proves
I've pinned him to his uniform, just the way,
this morning, I asked my daughter not to.

And now I'm standing in snow that creeps
above my suede loafers (*sigh*), among conclusions
of every make and fashion of car: hulks

hoisted into stacks, chrome bumpers
and greased axles filigreed with delicate
doilies of snow. How catholic—in the other sense
of *embracing all*—this final reckoning. And here, too,
individuals come, seeking that certain, errant part
that fits his errant need. Or hers.

Between the Lines

My daughter wants to draw on the misted glass
left by last night's rain; but it's cold, she says,
and pulls her wet fingers away. I have an idea,
and fetch a tapered paintbrush for her to work
her lines and dots and circles into what,
triumphant, she informs me is an elephant.
Hours later, at the coffeeshop, I follow the movement
of a window washer sponging suds on plate glass,
then sliding it off, methodically, with the squeegee.
This rapt attention on the grown man's face,
facing us inside, but focused on the glass,
is what I saw in my child's shoulders from behind,
in the tilt of her head, her lifted, moving arm—
and it's what I saw, I'm recalling now,

in this same coffeeshop, years ago. She looked
about twenty, seated on a counter stool, drawing.
Or rather, I noticed, she's coloring with crayons
in a coloring book. Why would she be doing that?
She's far too old—though old enough
she could be doing it with irony: a part
of something larger—art project, or theater set;
or maybe it's a kind of hands-on homework
for a childhood psychology class?
I sat down with my coffee, then saw, in the space
where her shirt lifted on her lower back, a tattoo
of an angel—no surprise there—but drawn
in the outline form of a cartoon coloring book.
And not filled in. Whatever guess I'd hazarded
about her coloring—childish, educational, or *uber*-hip—
gave way to a disturbing feeling I'd walked in
upon some private, necessary ritual.

The window washer wipes away the froth,
and I admire his practiced method: first,
cutting along the inside edge of the frame,
then in bold arcs, wiping the middle of the pane,

with a twist of the squeegee at every turn, in order
to catch the excess water, and leave no trace
on glass that's now transparently unfilled.
No glamour, not much pay—but I see that girl again,
and my daughter, as I watch him focus on his skill.

He works in just the way I'll teach my daughter
to fill the lines of coloring books, when she's a little older—
one skill, at least, I'll teach with confidence.
I've drawn and written numberless lines,
erased and filled them in and read between them;
drawn enough to know I'll never see
the entire picture of who we are. But I'll accept
the best that comes, by which I mean the most,
as much as best: that thrill I get, or see in someone else,
leaning into the act of making marks,
fulfilling and forgetting oneself at once.

When the Circus Comes

You can forget how dull it gets to be,
driving around on another cycle of errands,
until you mix in a couple of elephants.
And it's funny how instantly I recognize
and accept what I'd least expect to find
in a parking lot in a midsize prairie town—
but these sudden silhouettes, lithic shadows
standing like a Stonehenge outside the arena,
prevent all effort to see them as
anything but what they are.
                              Which is,
amazing. Even without the headdress,
the sequined lady riding the neck. Enough
to drive out here, kids in the backseat,
before the weekend's so-called greatest show, and behold
the routine of these elephants on the blacktop.

Milling about an unbound bale of hay,
they spread it around, using trunks like leafblowers;
or like pitchforks, tossing it on their backs;
now chopsticks, pinching delicate wisps to their lips.
And even before two trunks intertwine (What on earth
does *that* feel like?), we can sense their hold
upon each other. They love, says the man
who tends them with shovel and hose,
to have company. They look at us, it seems,
with the same regard we look at them. And so,
when one of them swings her head from side to side,
and moves her forefeet like an old soft-shoe,
with flourishes of her trunk's great baton,
it's easy to believe what I tell my small daughter:
Look, she's dancing.
                      But almost
in the instant of saying it, I remember
a film I once saw of that same movement,
and a narrator explaining this dance is a sign
of confinement, boredom—a kind of psychosis.

Yet they seem happy enough. Of course, you might say
the same about us, watching these elephants,
so willing to be transported
by creatures shipped here to fulfill
some desire we've been trained to forget.

Crying Dog

Again the neighbor's dog has roused me
from bed, barking and howling
like my own mind, now my sleep's
been breached, and I'm laid open
to all marauding thoughts and worries,
those workday grudges never failing to disturb
with that false, but dogged question:
*Why isn't your life a perfect orb
of happiness, self-contained and certain?*

Last month, in the coffeeshop,
I let myself complain to a woman
I knew, if not well, then more than slightly,
as I griped about work, the nag of committees;
and she listened, with sympathy, and barely
mentioned, in passing, she'd been a little ill.
Yesterday I read her obituary.
She must have known, and knowing, still
she listened. That is what I need to learn.
Listen: to the silence. Of death. My own—
its undistractable space that waits
beyond the barricade of petty thoughts.

And I try to conceive that silence
that contains no self to even hear it,
—but there goes the neighbor's dog again.
This time, his harrowing yelp taunts me
with a poem by Rumi, where a howling dog
is howling out of love for its master—
the howling is a kind of prayer,
but one that becomes its own answer,
giving voice to the love that is
its origin. But certain nights, I swear
I ought to kill that dog (the neighbors not
at home, so unavailable for murder);
and when I come to the fence to try

to quiet him, he melts with joy at my
approach, till I begin to love him.

All I do is close the curtains.
My livingroom—arranged and fretted
into order (even the cats like striped bolsters
on the couch), a domestic version
of that longed-for orb of happiness. Oh God—
can it be that what I really need
is that midnight-frantic, circling dog
to teach me how to cry—
that miserable dog, that windowbreaking cry?

II.

"I don't know about that, dear," said Miss Marple. "Very painful and distressing things happen in villages sometimes."

—Agatha Christie

The Assistant District Attorney
Quits His Job

Dear Sir—

Regretfully I must again submit
my resignation. Because you have refused
to accept my previous, I must assume
that further explanation is in order.
I'll put it this way: I would rather tender
my resignation than to be resigned
to lacking tenderness. A case in point:

A delivery man arrested Friday morning,
passed out in the front seat of his Budweiser truck.
Public Intoxication. Fair enough: he'd left
the motor running, a danger to himself and others.
My job should be a cinch, except for this:
just how, exactly, does a man end up like that?
He'd been a bartender, got married, wanted more
from a job—normal hours, benefits. He's 27,
new wife, a mortgage, baby daughter. Pressures.
So: maybe *one* beer, out of that whole truckload.
Well, maybe one more. And so it is they find him,
feet on the ground, head on the driver's seat,
like Pooh Bear stuck in the honey jar. I'm reading
those stories to Jessica at bedtime, and have come
to realize how much a life is built on stories.
The evidence suggests the man no longer
believed the story he had told himself:
that a steady job would make him a steady man.
But tell me, is that grounds for prosecution?

My daughter believes in Pooh, and there's a case
to be made for her believing. I believe
in the law, but my believing hits a wall
with these two robberies sitting on my desk:
a man who robs a Christian bookstore, and tells
the clerk that Jesus told him to; a kid holds up

a *What-a-Burger,* dressed in Batman cape and cowl.
We're going for armed robbery on the Jesus guy,
because he *said* he had a gun, although
he never showed it. But he also *said*
that Jesus made him do it. You see my point?
He didn't need the money; neither did the kid.
What they *needed* was Jesus, or Batman—
a story they could act upon. Behind it all,
the story that you'll tell come next election:
numbers of convictions you can feed the voters.

I wanted to believe the law is wisdom,
a nation's gathered learning. But it may be just
as much the written demarcation of
our failures—a kind of Latin chickenwire
reminding us how far we are from getting there.
And that's how stories are, because they never
really end; they're more about the wishing
to arrive. That's why Jessica will say, as soon
as the chapter on Pooh or Piglet ends,
"Daddy, read it *again.*" Don't get me wrong,
I still respect this effort that we call
the law, and I intend to practice still;
but in some setting where I'll really *practice,*
in the common sense: an athlete working on
his skills, a monk whose meditation takes
a lifetime; my daughter, stretching her small
fingers across the keys of the piano,
the white and the black, sounding out the chords.

Sincerely—

Steve

For a week now I've been thinking of a squirrel
a woman found in her garden, dead.
It made the local paper. What made it news
was this: a note tied around the squirrel's neck,
that read, *My name is Steve, and I need a place to live.*
What kind of joke is this, that lost its way,
and wandered into utter weirdness? Traveling,
I always notice that small boy at the gate—
do you know the one I mean?—
a nametag and ticket hung around his neck,
who stares at strangers as he waits to change
flights in an airport that is nothing
and nowhere to him. He is in transition,
which, he's learning, has something to do
with home—with leaving, or returning there,
with needing a place to live. And if you smile
in hopes of easing him, still he's on his own:
our inside warmest smiles can seem
like clown or gargoyle on the face's other side.
So little can he ever know of motives . . .
Now some I know are asking, what moves me
to be so moved by Steve?—the way I toss him in
to any conversation, to find out what the story means
to someone else, or if it just falls dead.
I know what *she* makes of it: "Harassment,"
heads the item in the paper. I picture her staring
squint-eyed behind blinds at neighborhood kids,
each one a suspect. But I suspect the answer
runs deeper: within the weirdness
of that squirrely act, I can't help but feel
there's something *normal* going on—normal, I mean,
for one who's lost connections, for a time:
the way you've seen them, panicked in the middle
of the street, running left, then right, then left,
as the wheels bear down. Surely you've seen them—
I know I have. The wheels, I mean.

Police Blotter

How many months?—Mornings
waking up sick; crying
over cabbages in the supermarket,
at her mother's house, at Mass;
indulging in the solace of ice cream,
feeling heavier in her shoes—
how long did it grow inside her,
this conception, before it came to light?

She must have cried when she wrote the letter;
it had to be a letter, written
by hand. And cried when he answered—
the husband who moved away last summer;
cried when he returned, out of love,
or duty, or both, and held her;
—but no further, that first night in bed,
because a woman is not ready, so soon after.

Next day, in the Neonatal
Intensive Care, where she showed him,
safe behind the viewing glass,
some dozen small faces,
how did she ever manage
to choose just one—which boy or girl
to lift his hand toward, her hand
on his wrist, and tell him,
Wave to your little baby?

I imagine the next two days,
the next two days were pure
belief—embodied in the rituals
of choosing infant wear, a bassinette,
a month's supply of smallest
Pampers, and the enormous, weightless fate
of a name. But there must come a time
to bring the child home. The truth
must have brought her to

her knees, such wailing and gnashing
as seldom heard outside the Emergency Room,
imploring the hard tiles, the bewildered nurses,
Where is my child? Her husband,
who had left the marriage and returned
to this questioning,
watched her as she told the detectives

of a monstrous crime, a kidnapping—
a monstrous, and a difficult crime,
no easier to accomplish
when there is no victim taken;
which is how I come to read
in nine slim lines
of the morning paper, of her arrest
for filing a false report.

What happens to her now
depends on whether she can make him understand,
that robed and gaveled judge,
that there was a crime,
a crime of someone stolen
away. Where is the lie
in the story, she might ask, if it brings you back
to what once was true?

The Night Shift

She didn't come to work last night—again.
Tonight, makeup thick as spackle, long sleeves
in July. A gold bracelet I've never seen before.
When our shift winds down to just a couple
of couples at corner tables, wanting
to be left alone, I tell her we girls
need to talk.

She says, "Of course I *want* to,
but he swears, if I do . . ."
The bracelet quivers as she lifts her glass.
"You're already at risk," I say: "Risk more
to save yourself." Which sounds good, saying it.

Then I hear the door swing open, and her face
freezes up. He's never come to her
at work. He's drunk—slack-faced, smiling,
all happy with himself. Damn good-looking,
I must say, and a charmer, too,
at first. Asks her sweetly, can he order
a drink, and I can see how she fell for him,
—that phrase we use for love, and lies.

But by the time our drinks are halfway
gone, it's like trying not to sweat.
We talk, she tells him I'm a painter.
"An artist?" he says. "You don't look like
you're starving," eyeing me up and down,
hungry. I'm about to let him have it,
when I feel his foot against my calf. No—
it's her foot. Her face a politician's grin,
her head shaking, No, please no. It's then

I know what I have to do. I smile,
the kind of smile you give the dentist,
offering your mouth to his fingers, his drill.
And I must listen to him—listen as

he tells her she should wear her hair more sexy
—like mine. Listen as he tells a filthy joke,
and at the punchline, squeezes *my* hand.

I feel, as if it were around my throat,
that hand; picture its closed fist against
my cheek, and now I'm *her.* I learn to follow
her example, saying nothing—my tongue tied
to a steel spring tensed inside his head.
I am part of his mechanism.

I stay, I smile as he teases me; I go so far
as to flirt with him, I so much need him
to feel good. When they leave,
her shoulders scrunched in his thick arm,
she floats a backward look to me,
a look of thanks, as if to say
it's alright, at least for tonight she'll be safe
at home with him. I lift
my hand to wave, then rub my wrist,
as if some new piece of jewelry
were hanging there.

Against Witness

One of us must have a gun,
I said.

Four cars stopped on a desert road,
it's only likely: statistics.

The horse that had been tossed
from the toppled trailer,
writhing, slammed his skull
teeth-first against tarmac.

It hurt so much
to watch: how can I presume
to write it down?

Two shots released him.
Blood. Urine. Shit.

A rope around the neck,
and four men trying to haul
1100 pounds off the road.

It would not give.

Stopping in Artesia

How many nights will you be staying?
—Motel Clerk

Out here you can tell a man's work
by his truck. But you're not driving a truck
past gas fields where the sulphur stinks
enough to make you renounce all lungs.
West wind saves this town, agitates among
junipers rooted in sand, each one holding
a shadow deep in its craw. Nobody
loves them, but at least they're good
at staying; not like oil, not like the price
of natural gas. The workday starts early, builds
to a big lunch. In the café, anyone can smoke
if they want to, and most want to. Do you know
the word *gas* comes from *chaos?* And the fire
that cooked your burger came from beneath your feet?
Afternoons are the hard stretch; the sun
the only thing beyond question. It cuts
a white acetylene blaze around the edge
of drawn curtains in your motel room,
while the swamp cooler rattles on the roof;
the road a diesel throb. Remember the junipers
will hold that shadow till nights come
moonless, and shadow swallows all.

Holy Saturday

Along the creek where they found the dead man,
papery disks of elm seeds
drop like scales, flecking the green

water. Coals of a pissed-out
party fire, beer cans, condoms,
syringes like scattered

nails: Is this what a world
looks like, its God killed and gone
to hell? Down here

is a place for sinners: deep inside,
though not quite a part of
the city; where I satisfy my urge

to watch returning
warblers probe and point among buds
tipping the oak twigs red

as souls turned into trees in the *Inferno*
whose limbs, when snapped, seeped blood.
How quickly my imagining of hell

turns formal—an artist's, a moralist's
place, where a God might send His Son
to fetch back something He regretted

having thrown away. The caught smell
of flesh-rot fetches me to the real
carcass of a dog, tossed

on a bank where, for centuries,
the buffalo, their cowled heads lowered,
had come to drink. Those herds were damned

along with Comanches who hunted them;
sprawled over by a city
where yesterday the clear sky darkened

with clouds of greenish, toxic smoke, sent up
from a burning scrapyard—cars, old tires,
gasoline & exploding batteries—stinging the eyes

and lungs of residents in nearby
apartments, a low-rent neighborhood
expelled, an evening in exile.

I wonder, if I were there,
would I have been thinking of things to save,
or if I myself might be saved?

Or just found—like the murdered man raised
out of this water, his naked skin showing signs
already of decay.

Flyover

At cruising altitude
    from a window seat,
the West Virginia woods
    seem a rumpled sheet
        of maroon, autumnal
Appalachian velvet.

Save here and there
    a whitish patch,
as if bald from wear
    or smudged with ash—
        and yes—there, on a hill,
a lit cigarette.

That is, a puff of smoke.
    (Once so common,
lighting up—a desirable chic;
    or so millions imagined
        before learning it would kill.)
Passing over, the jet

banks westward, and takes us
    to our intended, out-of-sight
metroplex in Texas
    shining in the night
        like glowing coal
—and burning it.

Driving Westward

Nightfall, ten miles out of Lovington,
a sulphury glow beyond horizon—
a rumoring, a looming, then a far apparition
of flame: small at first, match-like; then torch-like,
till, after miles, a literal pillar of fire.

Then I come to a reef of cars and pickups parked
in rows, as though a drive-in, or fireworks.
I stop the truck, drawn in—to watch, to ask:
a roustabout tells me it was a natural
gas well that blew, and a single spark
set off this firespout, four stories high,
three thousand degrees. Infernal: the blue
upward rush, the black-veined orange boils of it,
the surf-like explosion of air.

They tell me it's burned this way for days.
The steel rig, melting, bows toward the flame
flickering on the watchers' faces. No one
is talking, and none can do a damned
thing about it. But here I am, lingering,
one of the crowd, caught up in this rapture
of elemental fire, consuming us, as if this focus
were something we'd been waiting for.

Peaceable Kingdom

In her dream a hawk descended
on a rabbit, but as she watched it fall
—or no, she said, when *something* saw the hawk—
its wings lit up, the way a flag burns, edges in,
and then in amber light it flew away.
"What do you think it's about?" Her question hung
and disappeared. But I may have answered
(or *something* may) in another dream last night:
Walking again in Manhattan, though even in dream
the city's changed from when I lived there;
and so I'm always walking toward a place
I can remember, but can't remember *where*.
This time, she's with me, as an open space emerges
on the West Side—perhaps the trainyards where they hope
to build a stadium and lure the Giants back; or farther up,
closer to the river, where Audubon had owned
an estate in the 1840s, when passenger pigeons
sold by the bushel in barrows, and rails' eggs were harvested
by the hundreds in Jersey marshes. Or nowhere:
we walked down streets of brownstones and storefronts bent
in expressionist angles, tenements and blind warehouses,
girders of the elevated subway tracks, riverward
to the meadow where they lead the calves each evening.
Yes, the calves: in the dream it simply happens—
happens about three or four a.m., to judge
by the quiet of the cross-street curbside where we stood
(the same time in the meadow as the bed where I dreamt it)
looking across the long grass, brilliant, dewy under streetlight,
to the flocked shadows under trees, the Hudson's mussel-shell sheen,
where the brown calves shuffled, nose-to-tail, across.
In the meadow's pooled quiet, then, a lion's head
(dandelion? lionstooth? *dent-de-lion?*) lifted from the grass,
rose on haunches, stood; then another followed from below,
and more exotics rose beneath them, folding into one another,
a multifoliate, animal, animated flower:
some with jaws to throats, some at rest, surging and
diminishing, like swells of orchestral music, but silent—

In the morning, I told her where we'd been, dwelling
on the details, holding on to that place, or holding off
the question, "What do you think it's about?"
Something in the inner life of a man?
Of a man and a woman? Of a city? *Something*.
Its meaning may be nothing more than how
hard it was to let it go: each morning act—
making breakfast, putting on my clothes, carrying out
the trash—a kind of eyesore piece of real estate
erected on a sacred ground. And walking through
my day, I thought of that painting by Edward Hicks,
early American Primitive, of the lion and children,
wolf and leopard, oxen and sheep, gathered by a river
as, in the background, William Penn unfurls a treaty
among tall, bronze, feathered men. All of us have seen
that painting, or some version of it: because the painter,
a preacher, in love with Isaiah's vision of a country
redeemed of conflict, even human and snake,
had painted that scene over and over again,
nearly a hundred of them; because he could not stop
remembering what he'd seen—in a dream, perhaps?
Somewhere. By the time he died (Audubon by now
crippled and dumb from a stroke), he must have seen
how wrong it all turned out. The paintings change,
the animals harder to contain: the lion twists to arch
its back; the leopard bares its fangs; the children now
cower underneath the elm; or the bear
wanders off, hungry perhaps for something more
than the stalk of corn it had to share
with a cow; or one of them just lies down—
exhausted or bored stiff from yet one more
attempt to arrange and re-arrange, to preach
into harmony a composition that was just
too complicated to listen. And still, he kept on painting.

III.

Nature repeated its wise tautologies: a forest was a forest
the sea was the sea rock was rock
                                        —Zbigniew Herbert

From the Footbridge

Where mayflies metamorphose
from water born to airborne,
        briefly becoming both
morsel for fish and for bird, shared
        by rising trout and swallows diving;

where troutlip and birdbill meet
at the water's membrane, make
        perfect rings that, widening,
intersect, I wonder:
        is there a moment when,

beyond the aimed-at insect,
bird or fish might notice the other—
        or more—spy a whole realm
where they fly in water
        or swim in air?

Or is this a question only a person
would ask—my own face eyeing me,
        reflected in the dark
surface below, neither fish
        nor bird to break me up?

Carrizo Creek

Baudelaire walked through a forest of symbols.
The forest where I'm walking is literal.
But I am going fishing, which is never far
from symbol. Carrizo Creek is a mile long,
and a few feet wide. Fed with springs, it maintains
a wet crease in dry mountains, meandering
metaphor of a vein that still fishes,
while the larger stream that receives it,
barrened and battered in the cycle
of years-long drought and sudden flood
that's become, in our lifetime, our larger weather,
is being—literally—rebuilt by bulldozer
and backhoe. So: is my Carrizo Creek
symbolic of holding on? The undercut bank,
its roof of roots; shadows along the watercress:
small sanctuaries for wild brown trout, more
secretive and gorgeous than any browns I've seen.
Or hope to see: "True symbol
of the foolishness of hope," wrote Wordsworth
of the rod and line. I open the flybox
and choose, from many, this thing with feathers,
polypro, and rabbit fur, a metaphor
of the mayflies darning their eggs into
the water's surface film. Fishing's hard work,
it's patience; if nothing else, a study
in attention. How else, stalking away
from the stream and back to get
a better angle for a tricky cast,
would I find, dead among pine needles,
this palm-size span of an Io moth,
a beetle feeding upon it like a man
dressing a whale? My fingers spread open
its powdered wings, to reveal concentric O's,
irised circles, that correspond to eyes.

Consider the Hagfish

Avail oneself of carrion drift, the hake's, the haddock's,
the cod's slow plummet. Sniff them out and kiss
with tentacled lips that cannot close. Exude slime:
ease your way through anus, mouth, or gill
of the fresh corpse, or the barely living still;
writhe into the stomach, like an eaten thing,
and then begin to eat
with tooth-like tines of evertible tongue.

When gill-net comes, have no gills.
Suck guts of the gill-slung
until a bag of skin with you inside it,
"unmitigated nuisance," remains. Exude slime
to disgust the sea lion, then slip
from your self-surrounding sac
by tying your eel-like length into a knot,
and swimming through yourself.

"No true heart": a series of pumps shift blood
through boneless stretch of body, bordered
by a single wraparound flap of skin
for fin. For eyes, two lensless nodes to sense
vague whiffs of light. In half a billion years
leave but a single fossil behind. Know yourself
at your best when swathed in dead flesh:
your Atlantis, your palace, your Land of Cockaigne.

Departures

A spill of beads has fallen from a necklace—
Gigantic, slow, they spread across the park;
Or so it seems when, on your way to work,
You see a resting flock of white-faced ibis.
Binoculared, their wings hold jade and copper
Iridescence in the rinsed sun after rain;
Their crescent bills, stitching the moist lawn,
And curving necks are such that when a jogger
Comes crunching down the path, you want to stop her,
As if it were the greater indiscretion not
To gesture toward the birds Egyptians thought
Were sacred to the god of—but what's it matter?
They've risen now, and circle overhead,
These birds that once were judges of the dead.

Harbor Scene

In the dazzle of afternoon neon
of the new entertainment district,
we sipped rum at a patio table, overlooking
the chubby, fringed water-taxis

that hummed customers from one
attraction to another—theme bars and restaurants
(ours was vaguely "Pirate"), aquarium,
and mothballed, bunting-girdled warship.

Then, as if clowning for our pleasure,
a single water taxi began to spin
in tight circles and figure-eights.
There were only two on board—the driver

and a man who flailed a long-handled net
at something bobbing in the water, which,
when they drifted closer in,
turned out to be a bird.

The boat would sidle toward it—a cormorant,
I could see now—and the net lunge,
the bird vanish, to bob up again
on the boat's other side. Then we saw:

the cormorant had caught a fishing lure,
a long yellow plug with gangs of hooks
that hung in its beak, and snagged its wing,
wrenching its neck backwards.

We knew how the deadly game would play:
the man tried to net the bird,
while the bird—already caught once
and reeled to hand in agony

by some bewildered fisherman who
had cut the line—believed that fleeing

was its only chance to live.
But feathers of a cormorant don't have

the oils that keep a duck afloat;
and so each dive, each swipe of the net
brought them all a little closer
to the moment when exhaustion

and waterlogged feathers
would pull the bird below the waves
to stay. Its body swam lower and lower
as a small crowd of us gathered

and watched—keeping watch—on this scene
that had refined itself to simplest elements:
something needing to be saved,
and someone trying to save it.

"The Land's End"

—photograph by Jack Semura

Among the many birds
God tells Noah to harbor
in the medieval play

are fulmars. Creatures
of northern oceans, they shun
the land, nest on sheer

sea-cliff, earth's edge.
Abiding in wind,
slumbering on sea-swell—

how might Noah even hope
to catch one?
A lesser question, perhaps;

a greater one is why
the anonymous clerk who crafted
this mystery play to teach

unlettered peasants and townfolk
of England, would list
among redshank and rook

and familiar others
the far-faring, haar
and spindrift fulmar.

What vast arc
of love is this, that may be conveyed
in a human ark—

even as these fisted rocks,
upthrusts of earth's crust
giving perch to white seabirds,

are held, unblurred
amid savage surf, in the lens
of the artist's machine.

In Praise of Angus

Let us give praise to this old pony,
Shetland of thirty years, shaggy, big-bellied, a bit
swaybacked, who lets the child lead him
from the stall; who, locking his legs, allows her
to tug on the halter, and calling, smack
her lips to nudge him forward, that she may learn
his care—to brush and curry, keeping one hand always
on his flank so he knows; and never to touch
his feet, because he bears the fears from former abuse—
rodeo demons who used him as roping dummy.

Bought at auction for pity, Angus does not mind
the small weight of the girl in the saddle, and suffering
from congestive heart disease, suffers his heart
to rise to a trot. When I see him bringing my girl,
he brings, as well, all the millennia of animals
that are given us. I see not so much the *dominion*
granted by the Old Testament God; I see the granting
beneath it: I see in Angus the God who gave
not just the first world, but the choice
of learning to do it right; or do it wrong.

For the Coming Catastrophes

I stepped outside with a plastic bag of trash
for the dumpster, and just like that—
the MacGillivray's warbler in my backyard,
gleaning among new elm leaves.
I say "the" warbler, as if I've seen *him* before—
as if the planet's huge, impersonal tilt
toward spring, this random example of a species
moved by migration, were meant personally.
Still, I adore watching this one—his
shadings of gray and yellow-green,
his minute attentiveness, ever-moving.

I had been brooding on a news story I'd read
about the town where I was raised:
the story told how searchers found
a little boy's body wedged in a branch
at the edge of the Passaic River. He had swirled
down the rain-swollen currents, plunged
over the Great Falls in Paterson, from
the footbridge where his mother, because,
she said, she couldn't find a babysitter,
had dropped him in the water.
                              Later that night,
she checked herself into the same hospital
where I was born, recognizing her life was lost
in the same place where, by chance, mine began.

And I feel here a call to grieve; but can't—
me, who takes personally a migrating bird.
It's said that grieving, we really mourn ourselves.
I don't know. But I remember
my sisters and brothers and I, taking turns
to sit by our father as he was dying.
Delirious, he spoke to his own dead
brothers and sisters; he spoke to his children
as children—as if to keep us all, and always,
children, himself always father: *c'mon kids,*

he said, over and over, *c'mon let's go, let's get in the car,*
rounding us up, and bringing us all home.

When they brought the body of that boy,
in a plastic bag, back to the staging area
of the rescue effort, a small crowd had gathered,
most of them mothers. Nothing they could do,
little to say besides "How could this happen?"
Their question cannot *fathom*—that word
for the gesture of arms outstretched—
a mother dropping her boy in the river,
two persons they know about, but cannot know.

Maybe my father was grieving for his own
death in the names of his brothers and sisters,
of his children. Maybe it was me just mourning *me*
in his dying. I might believe that's so,
if by believing I can feel I'm more alive,
by calling to those I love. But when I hear
the prophecies of scientists, see live feeds
of floods, reports of drought, famine—plagues
of biblical dimension, but no godly cause,
though dimly connected to our habits,
like the power grid that brings these messages—
how to be anything but voiceless and alone,
short of calling to what we call divine?
A warbler. A father. But between them,
what attention, and what fathoms?

Bitter Lake

But for all its gesture
to the wild, nothing
comes more human

than this: "refuge,"
an oblong of mercy sliced
from the map.

Where hosts and dominions
of snow geese
billow and gleam

by water's edge,
I think of Lear, dead
Cordelia in his arms.

IV.

Love is between wisdom and ignorance
—Plato, *Symposium*

Love's reason's without reason
—Shakespeare, *Cymbeline* 4.2

Heron

That drought summer the lake hung low.
Once-sunken stumps hugged
their shadows, as we watched
a heron, across the water, articulate itself
in grave, measured strides, to where
a turtle slept on a log. The heron bowed
its fluent neck, its clever beak
nudged the turtle—slap into the lake!
In the story I wanted to tell,
the turtle was me, the water
that unreadable depth I feared,
and the heron, the heron was love.

Something underwater we couldn't see
moved the heron
to thrust—a frantic foot-long fish
speared on its beak. Lunging, splashing,
the heron bungled shoreward, flung the thing
on hard mud as if rejecting it,
then battered, batting and flipping it till
the beak raised skyward—
fish-head toward throat, fish-tail still writhing—
then a kind of backwards vomit, swelling
the long gullet. We watched, and wore
ourselves out with watching
the elegant wader reveal
an appetite so hideous—that heron,
that heron I had taken for love.

The Man Who Confuses Sex with Love

Even as, at times, I may shun them,
I recognize my various proclivities.
Though my doctor says it's wrong,
I sex a corndog, and sex a jelly donut;
and I sex Janis Joplin, but who doesn't?
Not that I'm incapable of refinements:
I sex that unctuous, oleaginous roll-
on-the-tongue that only the French can do,
of a *Premiere Cru* Chardonnay. Of course,
that's only "sex" in the vulgar sense,
not the real sex, as between
a man and woman, or brotherly sex,
or sex of God, sex of country.

Now love—love is another thing.
I first heard about love from a bully
down the block. When I made a sickly face,
he said, "Grow up, punk. Your parents
did it when they made you, and it's called *love.*"
As for my own history, I suppose
it's not unusual for having had love
with more than I have sexed.
Not that I was into casual love—
I'm terrified of picking up a lovably
transmitted disease; nor do I buy
into the notion of sex at first sight.

So confusing, so many competing messages:
are we "making sex" or just "having love"?
Just check out, if you can stand it,
the magazines by the checkout stand:
with the "Ten Love Secrets to Drive
Your Man Crazy," or every other month
another piece on how much love
is enough: how many times a month,
or week, or day, should a couple have love.

What's the point? If you're asking me,
I'd say that love isn't anything
we should feel we have to quantify.

Still, with sex, it's hard to tell
how long it will last. You think you know
what sex is when you find it;
you can't express it enough: at first it's all
love in the bathtub, love on the sofa,
love in the wouldn't-you-like-to-know . . .
Then when you're not looking, you fall
right out of sex. Then perhaps, it comes
you meet someone, with whom sex
and the work of sex are one: the sex carries on,
doggedly, through late nights at work,
the clogged drains and the mess on the floor,
the changing of diapers, the shots;
sex gets you through the supermarket,
the doctor's office, or mowing the grass,
fixing the roof, it's all underpinned with sex,
sex planted deep inside you, long-
lived and sturdy, pulsing and firm:
it burgeons, well into your withering.

Prenuptial

It is vain for you to rise up early, to sit up late,
to eat the bread of sorrows: for so he giveth his beloved sleep.
—Psalm 127

Lying in bed with you, not sleeping—sleep
the metaphor of all I want that's just
beyond me, that, when found, will prove a little
more than nothing. But you sleep. Your breath
is rich and satisfied, like something long sought,
now savored. We'll be married in a month.

For now, the late-night streetlight
pries at the blinds, at the eyes, proposes
to the waking mind a counter-metaphor
of marriage: all we want, and sure to come,
which when it comes will bring
a material rabble of gatecrashing thugs.
Junk mail, gunked-up drains, college deans,
the midnight voodoo of neighbors' howling dogs;
and worse, the after-midnight calls
announcing Illness, Stroke, and Tumor—
harbingers of that consummate moocher,
Death. We might as well invite them all
to eat our cake—they're coming anyway.

The dog we love has fleas. I hear him rise
and rattle. They're not metaphors to him.
He's right, the dog. What comes is real enough.
Like cold fusion, metaphor is much
to be desired, but hardly practical.
If two are one in marriage, it's often one
awake, and one asleep. And metaphor,
we learned in Shakespeare class, means "carry"—
as in, for instance, our dog carries fleas;
as in, tomorrow you will have my tiredness
to carry. Not what you had asked for, specifically;
but what you've chosen, choosing me.

And when it comes, my love, to carrying, there's none
with whom I'd rather carry on than you,
beside me in this marriage bed, mixed metaphor
we've made and lie in, where I want nothing more
than to stay, and wake in you, until
our little life is rounded with a sleep.

Hospital Room, 1 A.M.

An older woman rubs a younger woman's back.
Part of her job; but more:
she tells the younger woman how
she, in turn, can massage her child
to help her sleep. *You rub the lotion
in your hands to warm it up . . .*

The room is mostly shadow;
a small table lamp covered by a cloth
casts a sheen on outlines
of shoulders, working arms.
Asked, the older woman offers
something of her life.
And two surviving children . . .

The younger woman is my wife. Her wounds
are not from injury, but deep
and ancient as the sounds—
the wail and croon surprising even her—
she made through her pain of labor.

I lie curled on a chair,
father of one day,
and watch and listen. Your whole world,
everyone had said, will change.
I almost laugh: *My* world
now seems far
too small a thought.

I turn to the window—the city under storm.
Beyond snow roofs, the power plant
unfurls a plume of steam.
It curls in wind, breaks into clouds
I imagine into forms—
a rabbit, a mask, a pair of hands, and so on—
each form taking shape just before
it dissolves into the next.

Error upon Me Proved

A sound I hope to hear no more
than once—faint chime, small ring
produced by a wedding ring, rose-gold, flung
five flights to the cobbles of *rue Valadon*
from the closet-sized kitchen where, wrung
dry, come to the end of endurance and all sense
of possibility, I had thrown it out the window.

Hours later I'm walking by the Seine,
October sunlight, ardent blues and golds
on river and trees—the sort of light,
I remember thinking, at once so matter-of-fact
yet gorgeous enough to seem embellishment—
and I notice a young woman noticing
something glistening on the gravel path.

She bends, lifts it in her hands, and rising,
raises her eyes to mine, extending her hand
to show me, in it, a golden wedding band.
Perdu?—the only word I caught
from her question. How to tell her, yes,
I lost a wedding ring this morning;
but a different ring, and lost for good?
As I turned it over, she took my hand,
and curled my fingers around the ring, and spoke
in a fountain of French whose only words
I could discern were *evangeliste,* and *cadeau.*

The first word made no sense.
But when I heard the second word, "gift,"
in that moment I was ready to believe
in that magnanimous light bestowed upon us
for no one's acceptance or refusal,
believe in recovery, in what lies
nascent and curled within some clemency
of possibility. I could even think, holding that ring,

that she was what an angel *would* look like—nondescript
in denim and wool, no jewelry, canvas shoes,

and walking away . . . But then she turned,
eyes widening as she approached, speaking softly
in broken English now, yet unmistakable
in tone—a sincerity that marks the universal language
of fraud. Said she's hungry, has no
money for food . . .

And all this happened, as true as I've written it;
though I'd blame no one for disbelieving.
But I'd ask, why should my capacity
for gullibility be any less than another's
talent for deceit? I have to thank her,
who moved me from a failure to a fool.
My wife and I survived that trip;
but days afterward, returning to those paths,
I'd watch that same con played by others—
the fake finding of fake rings—
able, at least, to recognize what little I know,
how much I want to believe.

In the Place des Vosges

Hid below the rooflines' ridge, the sun
had raised a sort of alpenglow along
the brick façades across the square.

Eyes down, reading, I was unaware,
until the ring, forgotten on my hand,
began to glow, with rose and gold beyond

its own rose-gold. I raise my eyes—
there on a bench, in shadow grays,
my wife is reading. A beam of just-caught

reflected sunlight arrows a chestnut:
full boughs darkening behind her,
the inner limbs a blush of embers.

Ambition

I'm long past midlife, if only counting years;
but as for emotion, given my generation's
chronic childhood, I'm only now entering
my crisis, which I meet by cursing
my body's failings—constant ejaculations
about my sore knees, my afternoon need for a nap.

So my birthday arrives, at once expected
and unwelcome as another bill past due,
to be tossed on the pile with the others—
when in comes an email from a girl
I dated thirty years ago (no girl now:
she too, middle-aged, a parent)
and before I can finish the sentence that begins
"Just to wish you," I'm transported:

It's the corner of 86th and Lexington,
six o'clock on a midweek evening,
and I'm rising from the subway stairs.
We've planned to meet here, but even so,
the sight of each other thrills so much
we run and clasp in a kiss and hold that kiss
so long that when we emerge for breath,
we're startled by applause—clapping and cheers
from the crowd on the sidewalk,
the rush hour audience roused
to a standing ovation.

It was Broadway, I tell you—
it was goddamn Hollywood, only better:
with no help at all from director or script,
makeup, stylist, or lighting crew, no
personal chef, gaffer or grip, we had become
the heroes, *the lovers,* to whom it was given

to bestow this gift from the realm
of romance, and be given praise in return
for a moment that—surely?—must count for something
against all the moments I've since let go.

Counterpoint

From the livingroom radio, Fauré, long dead,
saunters in on whispering strings.

Making the last touch-ups to a new poem—
the only time, said Auden, to call oneself a poet.

Any minute now,
Jackie and Sophie will return from the pool.

I'm waiting to be interrupted.
Lucky as any man, waiting.

If I'm Reading You Right, Immanuel

Mid-spring, mid-afternoon, flecked shadows of half-fledged trees . . .

Compared to the book I'm struggling
to follow, how easy to surrender
to waxwings: their high-pitched corrugated whistlings
on the air, *in* it, as if the light had voice,
as if the chartreuse, scalloped unfurlings
of new walnut leaves were talking.

As if. The words distort, even as they tell me
what I see and hear. They lack the philosopher's discipline,
that well-regulated man of Königsberg, at his routine:
awake at five, in his nightgown at his desk,
a few coals on the raked fire for a trickle of heat,
as he writes, observing the pattern of his thoughts,
fine as the fractal frost on the panes that,
darkened, await the northern, late, winter dawn.
His days so orderly (it's said the housewives set their clocks
by his afternoon walks) that only thoughts and weather
seemed to change. A vantage, almost, pure.

Or so I might think, though my own thinking
mystifies his sentences—
the way an inside radiator's sighs
will fog to milkiness winter's precision of light.
And the waxwings, all the while,
sounding their single note. They fly
from holly to maple in straight lines—
like something I've just read: that *to draw a line in thought*
is to apprehend one thing after another; which means
one moment *must,* he says, *necessarily,* he says, depend
upon my holding of the moment before.
He called this thought an *a priori:* philosophy's reply
to *In the beginning,* whence all arises:
this phasing, this phrasing: the waxwings
singing themselves into becoming, riding on

their past. All this implication, this enabling—
the chiasmus of *when* and *now*.

Now then, by extension, as I sit in this garden,
am I not—*necessarily*—walking a sidewalk in Manhattan,
somewhere in Chelsea, near the comedy club
called Catch a Rising Star? It's audition night
and my girlfriend, who's nervous and prefers
an audience of strangers, will be on stage
for the first time, and I am forbidden to attend.
Two ways to please her, I'm thinking, two ways
to fail: one is to go in, one to stay away.
I contemplate disguises . . .

So then, now, if I'm reading it right,
that evening's walk is somehow requisite
to this moment in the garden: crossed
in the crossed limbs and shadows; hanging
in cap and dark glasses in the back,
in the crowd-fringe, the under-hedge
where jonquils hang their hooded heads.

Now, I say, and the word's round vowel holds
all my past. Still, there remains the problem
of all that's forgotten . . . the weather of
that evening (I think it was spring),
the faces of other walkers, closed to me now
as the storefronts' rolled-down metal doors.
And now, she and I are married

to other persons. There's a truth the philosopher
of Reason and Judgment never faced, who kept himself
away from Eros, and in this, too, was wise,
guessing that love leads us to disguise
the outer world with our inmost selves.
How, when I come to love it, the wheezy note
of the waxwing seems like a word:
"here, here, here, here," because *here*
is what I want to hear. Or when my wife
makes up our bed, and she kneels on the mattress

and draws the sheets and blankets toward her—
I think of the way a bird
finishes its nest, from the inside.

If I'm reading you right, Immanuel, it's clear
we can reason past illusions toward a wordless pure,
though I fancy, too, the tumble of my days
disappearing into one another, and love
that dresses and undresses them in words.
Words like *waxwings*. For Daedalus, they really worked:
rising, he saw the labyrinth below,
even as he'd drawn it in his thought.
But for Icarus, they are only *like* wings,
elaborate similes of what he craves . . .
I picture him, with a smile, flying,
just before he falls.

"The way a bird . . . ," I like to tell her
by way of chattering, exchanging words
that may be meaningless, but are enough to know
we're here to hear each other speak.
Like waxwings' whistlings, to tell us where we are.

V.

What I have to tell about the hereafter, and about life after death, consists entirely of memories . . .

—Carl Jung

The Story

My darling child, my only child,
whose memory at four years old
astonishes me—today you ask me
to take you back to that place
where there were stones, you say,
and flowers. And I hear
enchantment in your voice—
even if I can't recall
whatever it was that thrills you
when you say, *and crosses
on the stones, and praying hands.*
But with those words, I know:
where else but the cemetery
we walked through last May?
Yes, that morning sunlight,
warblers and orioles, returning . . .
But I'm not ready—my darling child,
my only child—to go there now;
to bring us to the story
beneath those charming stones.

Impromptu Novena in Mid-September

Understand the light, then, and recognize it
>   *—Corpus Hermeticum*

>   Memory is a kind
> of accomplishment
>   —William Carlos Williams

I.

Birdsong on the book page, birdsong on the brown rug;
fanfare of birdsong above the radio orchestra;
birdsong in shafted light of the wooden blinds.

In one moment I heard them—by which I mean
they'd all along been singing, building in my ear,
but only just then, my brain embraced what it heard—

all the neighborhood birds, a seamless textile of song.
Ordinary song, but not the ordinary time for singing—
was it something to do with sunlight, returning this afternoon

after days-long cloud-dregs of a distant hurricane?
Maybe there's a cause; but cause belongs to time.
What I heard was other than time.

II.

A vow I made this year, lost with the book of butterflies.
Or mislaid. I'd vowed to learn their names.
But now the backyard flickers with the strobe of their wings,
lavender, cream, and butter, orange, black and gold,
nosing about the shrubs, or with a single wingbeat rising over the fence—
a dozen or so of the same kind, preoccupied with our oak tree
(Is it the "sweets," as the tree man calls the sap from the broken limb?)
And in my head a flurry of names I like—
sulfurs, cabbage whites, fritillaries, checkerspots—
but cannot link with the actual butterflies around me.

Funny, but I feel
as if I'm trying, from this attention
to insects' small motions, to piece together
evidence, to make an *argument:*
for what I know—that I am moved to these creatures
because they assuage some ache I cannot name;
against what I also know—that much of our knowing
is also the source of pain.

The rebuttal of butterflies . . .

But the angled hands of my wristwatch interrupt—
it's time to fetch my daughter home
from nursery school; to stake a modest claim
on the future tense: a flowering plant we recently bought,
still bucketed on the porch.
We'll dig a hole—or I'll dig, she'll watch
and poke with a pink toy shovel—
and we'll plant the flowering lantana, more commonly known
as butterfly bush.

III.

This afternoon, light spills on the trees,
the trees spill shadows beneath them. Just enough mist
for air to be liminal, silvery. Leaves steeped in light.

And that soil-leaf smell—the just-mowed lawn in the arboretum,
the rain stored within, released to the sun—a scent that spells me
from my comfortable exile here in the southern plains, and summons back

the autumn leafmold and grassy scent of earlier places—
mountain trails, or wooded lots not yet gutted for houses or parking.
Memory, they say, is most vividly triggered by scent;

and why not? The molecules are *exactly* the same. Descending the steps
to the cellar of a London bookshop—it's the basement of my childhood,
bluegray light from the window wells, my father's workbench.

Not nostalgia—but elemental remembrance. How this late season,
summer dismantling itself, writing its own elegy in gorgeous lightfall,
presses me with that mingled moral of presence and loss: ashes

of my mother, my wife away for a week, my daughter an afternoon,
and shimmer of wavelight on a duck's breast, sheer electric streak
of blue damselflies in the lilypads—all these—crystallize, and cut.

IV.

I follow motions of a migrant warbler
feathered in drabs of olive and gray, disguised
as the underside of trees it probes in mid-September.

So precise—
the way the needle beak extracts
gnats, beetles, tiny flies

from underleaf and crease of bark—an effect
I've always likened to embroidery;
though, watched for long, it's not so exact

a match, for this flitting so indirectly
from limb to limb, or between the trees
suggests another analogy:

I think of Socrates,
how his questions crept from casual
pleasantries, to overarching verities—

as sleep, he'd say, compares to being full
awake; or as the soul, scrambled
with body, compares to the soul eternal.

So what sort of a sampler
(to follow my earlier line
of thought), would the needling beak of this warbler

have stitched, if its movement through time
could remain visibly evident
like a bright thread carried behind

the bird as it goes, obliquely intent,
from twig to twig, tree to tree, backyard, park, mountains, and further—
the whole downward slope of continent—

as if time were its own rememberer?

V.

Hardly the norm, the enlargement of these afternoons,
this charmed light. More to be expected
is more like yesterday: the mail as usual,
the white and blue van parked before my house,
as usual. Only this time, an SUV pulled up behind—
four men emerged, with nametags and clipboards,
and followed our letter carrier on her rounds.
Experts, no doubt, here to time
the footsteps, to reduce to a ratio of seconds
per house, the real-weather work of Sherri,
our mailman (so to speak)—who knows our names.

And most of what gets mailed is forgettable—
bills and advertisements, "throwaways" and "junk."
Still, I thrill at the mail's arrival, remembering
writing letters by hand, receiving them
from others: thoughts written in the past, calling
at my door. *Anamnesis,* an un-forgetting,
the return of someone held dear . . . "Dear,"
that salutation of past to present;
but maybe I'm pushing it—the metaphor,
the memory—were it not for the presence,
this memory pressing upon me all day,
of a friend I once knew, and could have known better.

A letter that came, decades back, with a newspaper clipping.
Not from him, but about him: murdered in Prospect Park.

Dear Fenton from Brooklyn—Fenton,
with tombstone teeth and half-hunched shoulders
and glasses mended with a bandaid—ungraceful frame
that bespeaks an inner magnitude, as though strained
by the freight of soul. Fenton who came shyly
to our habit of clowning, but then came to joy in it,
cracking up our friend Mike and me as we'd wait
for rock concerts beneath the faded remains
of painted vaudeville signs on the high brick façade
of the old Academy of Music . . . He went on
to study theology at Fordham; and we fell
out of touch . . . until the letter I received from Mike,
with a small item from *The Daily News,*
which as I read opened up like subway doors:
Fenton, stabbed to death, bloody, and wearing
a red dress, stockings, heels, lipstick and liner.
Carefully he must have prepared, that Saturday night,
and sauntered to the darkest part of the Park—which is to say,
he walked into the garden, knowing he'll be killed.

Asking, somehow it feels to me now, to return.

VI.

Even the evenings won't leave me alone: dreaming, I rise
          to this weather, its bluegold light, the sun angled
like an artist's brush, burnishing the glint of leaves, deepening
          the shades, even to the blades of grass we walk on:
a crowd of us wearing dark suits and dresses, in a band of meadow, wild
          with lilac and tiger lily, that somehow lies beneath
the Palisades on the Jersey side of the Hudson.
          Greengray water silvers downriver in steady breeze,
and I can see wharves and ferries of Hoboken, highrises of Manhattan—
          each one distinct in the special handling of the light.
I mean to say, it's the rural past folded into the past
          of the industrial port, folded again into the slick
co-ops and office towers of today: time refracted in itself
          like waves of sunlight in river waves, seen underwater.

Whatever one thinks of dream logic, those occult convolutions,
        its rhetoric is redundancy: the feeling
of being here persuades me I'm here. And the feeling
        of recognition, as if this grassy level along the river,
where a crowd of us are walking toward a chapel,
        has come to seek me out, has returned to me.
And my father hurrying there, black suit and tie, starched white shirt,
        steps toward the riverbank, and I see
he is walking barefoot—and so I discover
        it's his own funeral we assemble for. Is that why
he hurries? He seems to know more than anyone
        why we're here, this old man hauling nine decades behind him.
The haul has frailed him. I want to help him cross
        the rougher grass by river's edge, so I push through the crowd;
but as I reach him he is already falling, straight
        as a hammerstroke; but slowly—the moment exploded
by my own adrenaline surge. No splash—
        then underwater, a swift sliding deeper, like flight.

VII.

The descent beckons
                as the ascent beckoned
                                —How
can I not read those words, when I sit down this evening
under a tent of lamplight in the livingroom,
with borrowed iPod and ear buds, to record
poems for a colleague in the hospital?
I used to pass him in the supermarket,
among vegetables or fish counter, and we'd pause
to admire our two-year-old daughters, one red, one blond,
each like a lotus blossom sitting in the cart.

We both love William Carlos Williams—*Spring and All*
his favorite book, and mine. Now, the hidden growth
growing inside him, pressing against
his brain, leaves him medicated and bedridden,
unable to read but hoping for news

that, if not better, may stop getting worse.
So I'm leafing through a book of poems,
looking for words that might cover the stellar distance
between my ordinary expectations
(reading and waiting for the mail,
and later to stroll my daughter to the playground)
and the unsuspected place where he's arrived.

I imagine I can draw the whale's belly as well as anyone—
no moralized, gothic vault of ribs, no *place,*
but a cramped surround of muscle, acid, and brine,
utterly lightless. But what makes me think
I could address my colleague's need? Only this, maybe:
that Jonah found room there for prayer. I remember
in the dream, when my father's white feet,
the last of him, slid beneath the chill water, I did not hesitate at all
to dive in after him, to that polluted river the dream
would not let me, even in full dive, reach.

VIII.

Seed pods of the locust tree,
leather-brown question marks in the grass.
In shadow, the grackles
seem like black holes; in sun,
small pavilions of iridescence. I am trying to understand
another afternoon of manic light—
affecting light, connecting somehow to affection.
But does it *mean?* Or is it only
my damn feelings flattering me again?

Would I feel this way if I'd gone a day without food?
Would I feel this way if I were the man waking in a hospital bed?
Would I feel this way . . .
                              —Except that the sun
rebukes the subjunctive: it is the strident voice of the present tense,
raging on the blades of grass, amid the leaves, against the clouds:
this is the present, so full it cannot be contained. Touch it
and it spills over into the past—not escape from the present,
but the past emerging, where it has always been,

bearing upon us—and by *us* I mean myself and the loves I call forth;
this is remembrance raised up
to sacrament; this is the ancient word, *anamnesis:*
calling forth the past, and the past in its willingness
to come forth, to ask of us: *Do this*
in remembrance of me. And circled at a table,
my family at suppertime, father and mother who are gone
                            now, sisters and brothers
who are older now, widowed, divorced and remarried,
                            grandparents now—
but all that yet unhappened, hidden in the future invisible
at this table set in the past, and waiting:

heart's blood, and the leaves in the windwaves,
green at rest, glittering in the surge;
the beat of wings above flowers, blue Russian sage,
wings in the ribwork of limbs, or to and from the lawn:
these are the *ways* we are given to see, our secular anamnesis,
immensity pressing on us, with a particular face;
these are the details that focus this present
that brims into past, the past passing back to me now.

IX.

This afternoon a cold front crowded in, sky overtaken
by hulks of clouds, deep-bellied and dull-sheened,
unpolished armor in a museum hall.

And isolate drops of rain, little ice-kisses.
Leaves taken, letting go. Equinoctial
September, passing. Sun the same angle as March,

striking not bare limbs, but the full flourish
of leaves. *Heart's blood, and the leaves in the windwaves.*
Passing, as I knew it would . . .

Night outside my window, barely opened
the width of a mail slot; the chill song
of a single cricket, slow.

What had come unbidden, or as if they willed it—
the dead walking again, anamnesis—now held
at a distance, only touchable by thought, flawed instrument.

I was looking up Jonah the other day,
and the thin pages of the bible slipped
from my fingers, to a psalm, where I saw:

This knowledge is too wonderful for me;
it is high, I cannot attain to it.
So these days were—what?—should I say, *heightened?*

They came like that psalm: without my looking for them,
and bearing the thrill that what's revealed
is revealed by something further hidden, and greater.

Thought, flawed instrument, pokes at this pearl:
Wonder conceals. Thinking and going nowhere, I fall back
to gratitude, wonder's residue.

Acknowledgements

Poems from this volume have been published in the following journals:

32 Poems: "Departures"; *The Common:* "Error upon Me Proved"; *Greensboro Review:* "The Assistant District Attorney Quits His Job"; *Hopkins Review:* "Crying Dog"; *Image:* "Impromptu Novena in Mid-September"; *ISLE:* "Harbor Scene"; *The Literary Review:* "Holy Saturday"; *Literature and Belief:* "The Call," "From the Footbridge," and "Monuments,"; *Ninth Letter:* "Consider the Hagfish" and "For the Coming Catastrophes"; *Northwest Review:* "Parable of a Birthday" and "Between the Lines"; *Open City:* "Against Witness" and "Stopping in Artesia"; *Orion:* "Driving Westward" and "Bitter Lake"; *Poetry East:* "Steve"; *Poetry Ireland Review:* "A Lesser Story"; *Salamander:* "In the Place des Vosges"; *San Pedro River Review:* "Driving Westward" (reprint); *The Sewanee Review:* "The Story"; *Shenandoah:* "A Cedar in Paris"; *Smartish Pace:* "Peaceable Kingdom"; *Southern Quarterly:* "Flyover" (under the title "Over the Mountain and Through") ; *The Southern Review:* "Heron," "In Praise of Angus," and "Prenuptial"; *Stand Magazine* (UK): "Hospital Room, 1 A.M"; *Tar River Poetry:* "Police Blotter" and "The Night Shift"; *Tin House:* "The Man Who Confuses Sex with Love"; *upstreet:* "When the Circus Comes"; *The Yale Review:* "Ambition."

"Heron" was published in *Pushcart Prize XXVII: Best of the Small Presses* (Pushcart Press); "The Land's End" was published in *Open to Interpretation: Water's Edge* (Open to Interpretation); "If I'm Reading You Right, Immanuel" was published online at *The Language Exchange: writing on history, language, and contemporary culture* (pages.slc.edu/~eraymond/ccorner/); "In the Place des Vosges" was reprinted on *Poetry Daily* (poems.com).

My thanks to editors who lent their skills to the above poems, in particular Phillis Levin and Jessica Greenbaum. My deepest gratitude to poets who have read these poems and the book in earlier versions: Bruce Beasley, Robert Cording, Jeffrey Harrison, Jacqueline Kolosov, and Daniel Tobin.

JUN 0 3 2016

CPSIA information can be obtained
at www.ICGtesting.com
Printed in the USA
LVOW12s1759290316

481260LV00006B/625/P